NY IS FOR NEW YORK

Haringey Libraries	
TT	
Askews & Holts	06-Nov-2017
428.1	
	3400022014

NEW JERSEY

H

V

W

L

SOHO

TRIBECA

FINANCIAL
DISTRICT

X

STRAND
BOOKSTORE

McNALLY
JACKSON
BOOKS

D

CHINATOWN

S

LITTLE
ITALY

B

LOWER
EAST SIDE

EAST
VILLAGE

BROOKLYN

C

CONEY
ISLAND

J

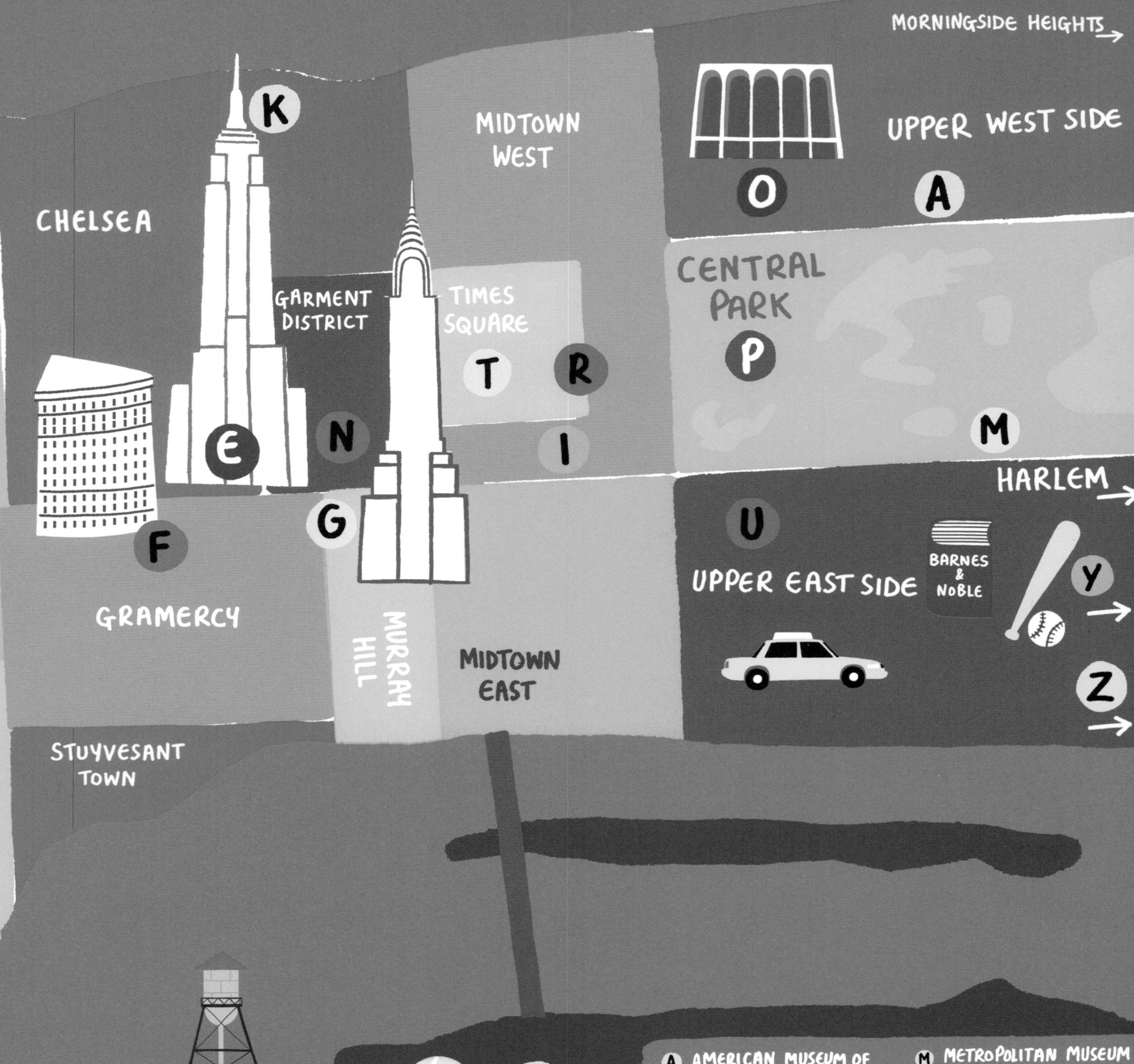

QUEENS

- A AMERICAN MUSEUM OF NATURAL HISTORY
- B BROOKLYN BRIDGE
- C CONEY ISLAND
- D DOWNTOWN
- E EMPIRE STATE BUILDING
- F FLATIRON BUILDING
- G GRAND CENTRAL TERMINAL
- H HIGH LINE
- I ICE SKATING
- J JFK AIRPORT
- K KING KONG
- L LADY LIBERTY
- M METROPOLITAN MUSEUM OF MODERN ART
- N NEW YORK PUBLIC LIBRARY
- O OPERA
- P CENTRAL PARK
- Q QUEENS
- R RADIO CITY
- S SUBWAY
- T TIMES SQUARE
- U UPTOWN
- V GREENWICH VILLAGE
- W WATER TOWERS
- X STOCK EXCHANGE
- Y YANKEE STADIUM
- Z BRONX ZOO

For my mum and for Marie-Louise

HODDER CHILDREN'S BOOKS

First published in Great Britain in 2016 by Hodder and Stoughton
This edition published in 2017

Text and illustrations copyright © Paul Thurlby, 2016

The moral rights of the author have been asserted.
All rights reserved.

A CIP record for this book
is available from the British Library.

ISBN: 978 1 444 93070 2

10 9 8 7 6 5 4 3 2 1

Printed and bound in China

Hodder Children's Books
An imprint of Hachette Children's Group
Part of Hodder and Stoughton
Carmelite House
50 Victoria Embankment
London
EC4Y 0DZ

An Hachette UK Company
www.hachette.co.uk
www.hachettechildrens.co.uk

King Kong 1933 Film © RKO Pictures

NY IS FOR NEW YORK

PAUL THURLBY

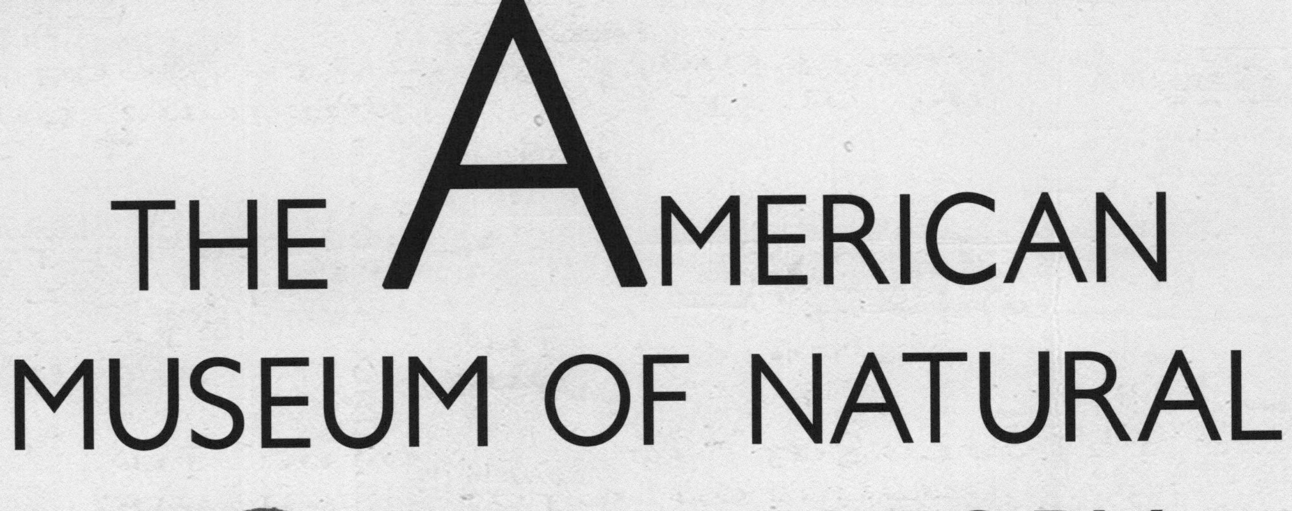

THE AMERICAN MUSEUM OF NATURAL HISTORY

is one of the largest museums in the world. It contains over 32 million specimens, including plants, humans, animals and fossils.

Its collections include dinosaur fossils, Ancient Chinese robes, and hippo skulls.

AMERICAN MUSEUM OF NATURAL HISTORY

BROOKLYN BRIDGE

It was the first steel-wire suspension bridge constructed.

is one of the oldest bridges in the United States. Completed in 1883, it spans the East River to connect the boroughs of Manhattan and Brooklyn.

Coney Island is the original amusement destination in New York. Over one million sun-seekers head to the beach on a summer's day.

Coney Island holds an annual hotdog-eating contest.

CONEY ISLAND

DOWNTOWN MANHATTAN

has a diverse community and a vibrant nightlife, and attracts many artists and musicians.

Favourite places to visit include Tribeca, Chinatown and Little Italy.

LAW OFFICE
QUICKLY
快可立
Bubble Tea
Slush
Juice
Cream Cake
BobaLife NYC
QUICKLY
川外川
FAMOUS
SICHUAN
KONG
SNAX
川外
FAMOUS
SICHUAN
川外

DOWNTOWN

THE EMPIRE STATE BUILDING

is a 102-storey skyscraper and stands at a total of 443 metres high. Opened on 1 May 1931, the whole structure was built in just 410 days.

It has 1,860 steps and 73 lifts!

EMPIRE STATE BUILDING

THE FLATIRON BUILDING

is one of New York's oldest skyscrapers. It has 22 floors and is as skinny as it looks. It derives its name from its resemblance to a clothes iron.

The Strand Bookstore, on the way to the Flatiron district, is home to 18 miles of new, used and rare books.

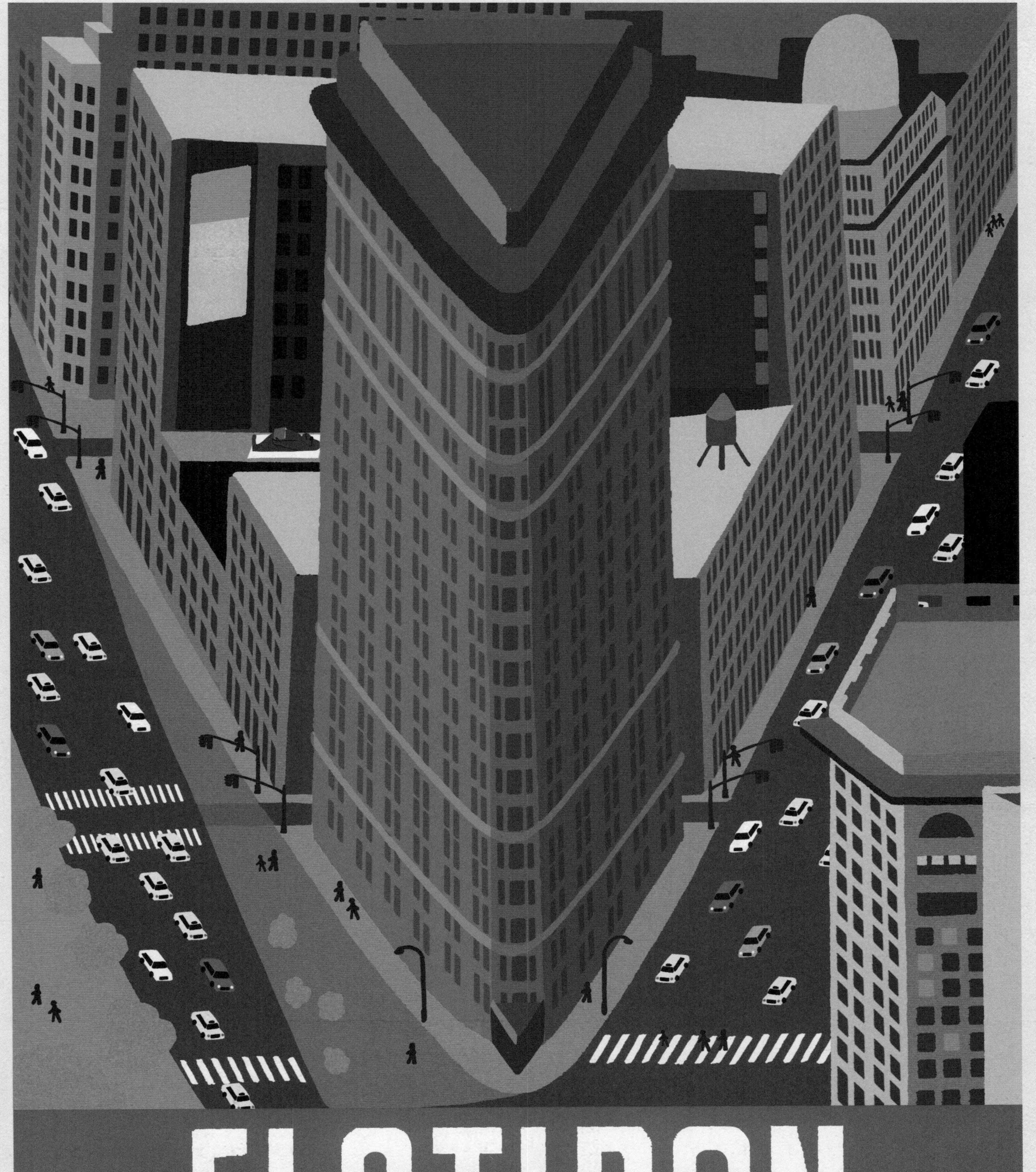

FLATIRON

GRAND CENTRAL TERMINAL

is one of the largest railway stations in the world. It has 44 platforms and 67 tracks, more than any other railway station.

The Chrysler Building is next door to Grand Central Terminal. It is considered one of the most beautiful pieces of art deco architecture in Manhattan.

The Grand Central clock is New York's most famous timepiece.

GRAND CENTRAL
TERMINAL

The High Line is a 1.4-mile-long park built on a disused railway track. This cool promenade has been redesigned and is now surrounded by trees and plants. It allows locals to take a traffic-free walk above the busy streets below.

HiGH LiNE

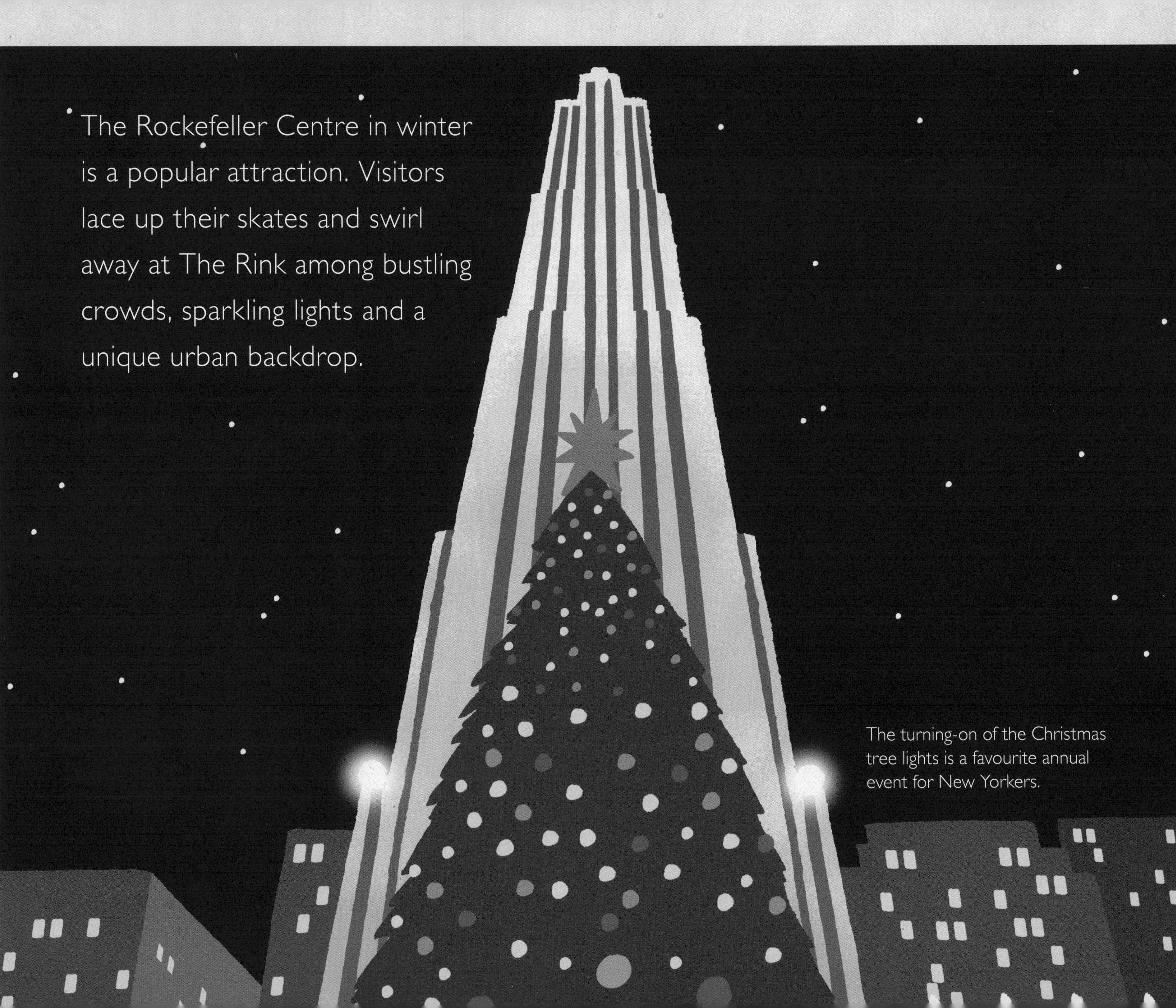

The Rockefeller Centre in winter is a popular attraction. Visitors lace up their skates and swirl away at The Rink among bustling crowds, sparkling lights and a unique urban backdrop.

The turning-on of the Christmas tree lights is a favourite annual event for New Yorkers.

ice skating

JFK AIRPORT

is the busiest international airport in the United States. It is home to six passenger terminals, four runways and over 70 airlines!

JFK wasn't always named after the former president, John F. Kennedy. It was originally known as Idlewild Airport before being officially named New York International Airport in 1948.

JFK AIRPORT

KING KONG

is a landmark black-and-white film about a gigantic gorilla called 'Kong'. In a memorable and terrifying scene, he escapes his captors and climbs up the Empire State Building only to fall dramatically to the streets below.

Ann Darrow is a fictional character with whom the giant ape falls in love. She is played by Fay Wray in the 1933 movie.

KING KONG

LADY LIBERTY

(also known as the Statue of Liberty) is an icon of freedom and of the United States. The statue is almost 93 metres high and was given to the people of the United States by the people of France in 1886.

The statue's crown has seven rays because the world has seven seas and seven continents.

LADY LIBERTY

THE METROPOLITAN MUSEUM OF ART

(known as The Met) is the largest art museum in the United States and among the most visited art museums in the world.

The Little Fourteen-Year-Old Dancer is a sculpture by Edgar Degas of a young student of the Paris Opera Ballet.

METROPOLITAN
MUSEUM OF ART

NEW YORK PUBLIC LIBRARY

opened in 1911 with a collection of over one million books. It now has 88 miles of bookshelves and 10,000 new books come in every week.

A famous scene in *Breakfast at Tiffany's*, starring Audrey Hepburn, was filmed in the library.

NEW YORK
PUBLIC LIBRARY

THE MET OPERA HOUSE

has nearly 4,000 seats and is the largest purpose-built opera house in the world. Its innovative programme of new and classic opera has helped keep it alive for more than 100 years.

The opera house got its start when a group of millionaires clubbed together to build a new opera venue.

OPERA

Central Park is the most visited urban park in the United States, as well as one of the most filmed locations in the world. With its lawns, trees and lakes, it is popular for sports and concerts.

CENTRAL PARK

QUEENS

is the largest in area of the five boroughs of New York City. One of its attractions is Flushing Meadows Park, home to the New York Mets baseball team and the US Open tennis Grand Slam.

Serena Williams shares the record for the most titles won at the US Open with Chris Evert.

QUEENS

RADIO CITY MUSIC HALL

is an entertainment venue that hosts concerts, stage shows and film premières. The art deco music hall opened to the public in 1932 and has 6,000 seats for spectators.

The gold stage curtain is the largest in the world.

RADIO CITY
Music Hall

The all-time annual ridership record is 2.1 billion passengers, set in 1946.

The subway is an essential part of city living in the Big Apple. There are 660 miles of track in use for passenger service, with a further 186 miles of track used for storage and transit.

evator to B D F M
Uptown A C E
center of platform
SUBWAY

Times Square is one of the world's most visited tourist attractions, drawing an estimated fifty million visitors annually. It is brightly adorned with billboards and is the hub of the Broadway Theatre district.

TIMES SQUARE

Upper Manhattan includes some of the city's most iconic locations such as Central Park and The Guggenheim Museum.

UPTOWN

GREENWICH VILLAGE

Most streets in Manhattan are known by their numbers, but the streets in Greenwich Village carry names.

is often referred to by locals as simply 'The Village'. It has retained much of its charm and historic character over the years. It is an artists' haven and has some of the best cafés in New York.

WATER TOWERS

are dotted along the skyline in New York. They may look like relics from a bygone era, but most New Yorkers still drink and bathe using the water stored in them.

Most buildings in the city taller than six storeys need some sort of water tower because water pressure is so low.

WATER TOWERS

THE STOCK EXCHANGE

is at the heart of America's financial industry. Trading opens at 9.30 a.m. every morning when the opening bell is rung. The closing bell is rung at 4 p.m. to mark the end of trading.

Nelson Mandela, Robert Downey Jr and Spider-Man have all rung the opening bell.

STOCK EXCHANGE

THE YANKEE STADIUM

is the home of the New York Yankees baseball team. The fans are some of the loudest and most knowledgeable you will find anywhere.

The stadium seats 57,545 people for baseball games.

Yankee
STADIUM

BRONX ZOO

is among the largest metropolitan zoos in the world, with some 6,000 animals, representing about 650 species from around the globe.

The zoo includes 265 acres of parkland through which the Bronx River flows.

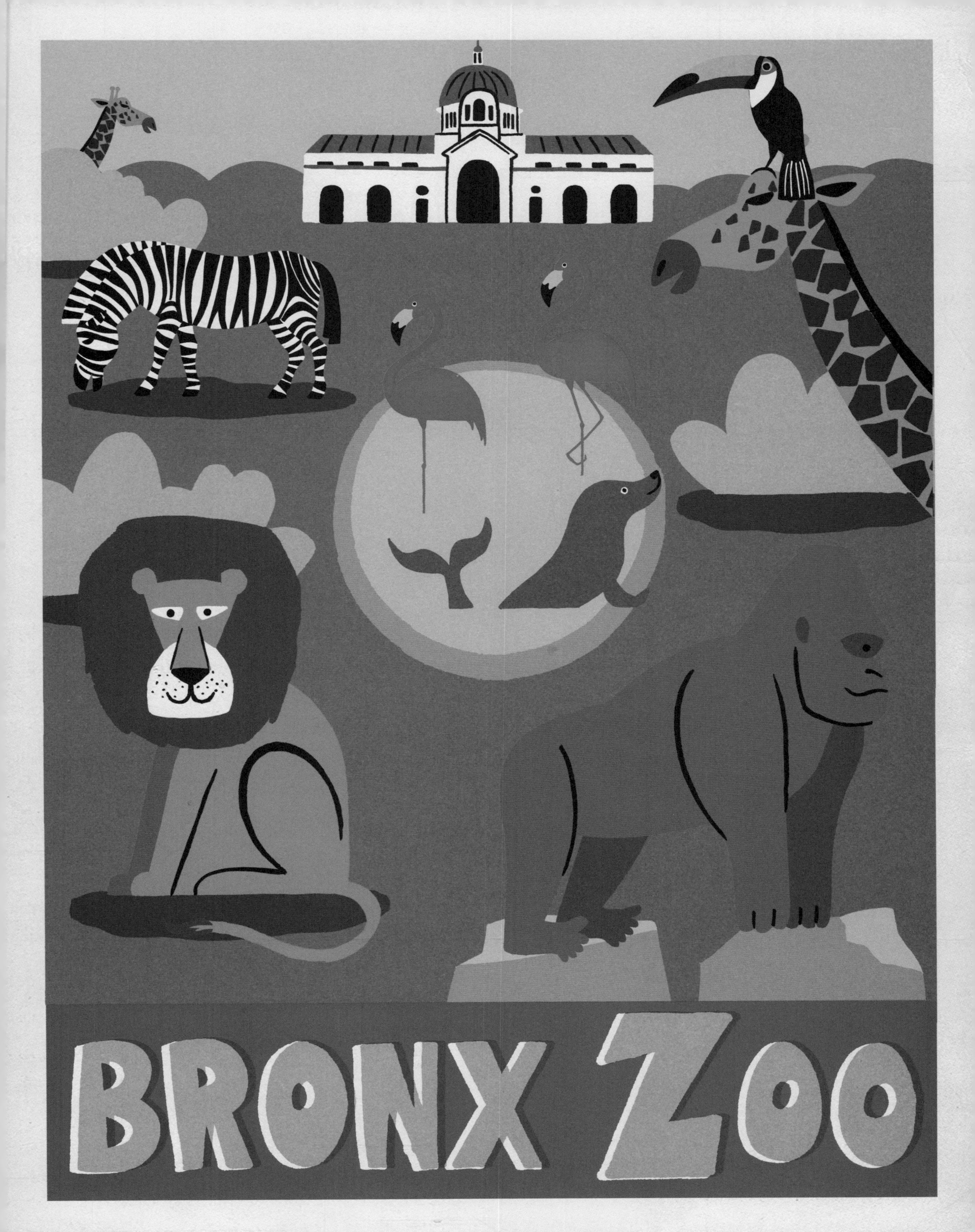
BRONX ZOO

In September 2015 I first visited New York. Just like that trip, making this book has been a great adventure. For me, using the alphabet is simply a way of structuring the book. From there, I expand on each image and tell the reader more about The Big Apple, taking in some of New York's most famous landmarks and streets.

When in New York, I visited the Empire State Building twice, once at night and once early in morning. It's a special place because a movie star gorilla once climbed up to the top of the building! Can you spot a gorilla on every spread?

Originally from Nottingham, now based in London, I have been a full-time illustrator since September 2006.

I'd like to thank my junior school teachers for seeing that I could draw and write well, despite holding my pen differently, and for recognising that there is no set way of doing things.

I've built up an impressive list of commissions working in advertising, design, publishing and editorial for clients including *The New Yorker,* BBH New York, Mother London, The French Tourist Board, Penguin USA, Ted Baker, Warner/Chappell Music, *The Washington Post,* Pimm's, Sarson's and The Southbank Centre, London.

Winning the Bologna Ragazzi Opera Prima Award in 2013 for my first book, ALPHABET, was one of the proudest achievements of my career so far.

Paul Thurlby

STOCK EXCHANGE

QUEEN'S

Tennis on other spread?

BEAUTIFUL BOOKS BY PAUL THURLBY:

For fun activities, further information and to order, visit www.hachettechildrens.co.uk